"David and Jonathan are wrestling with a serious problem here, and they give biblical advice that is full of grace and full of Jesus. Very concise, too, and that, too, is a virtue. Anyone thinking about going to seminary will benefit greatly by spending some time with this book."

John M. Frame, J. D. Trimble Chair of Systematic Theology and Philosophy, Reformed Theological Seminary, Orlando

"This book makes me angry and sad—because I wish it had been written years earlier. As I read it, I can see faces of people I love who wrecked their lives in seminary, and I wish I could go back in time and hand them this volume. Some of them lost the faith. Some lost their families. Some lost their integrity. The Devil wants to bring down ministers of the gospel, and he usually erects the demolition scaffolding in seminary, when we're too occupied with Greek flash cards to see the shadow of the pitchfork on the wall. This book, by brilliant men of God, can help you lay out a war plan. Read it, and fight."

Russell D. Moore, President, The Ethics & Religious Liberty Commission, Southern Baptist Convention

"Written by two men fresh from the trenches of theological education, this little volume is sure to help the new seminary student navigate the pitfalls of misplaced priorities, overcommitment, undercommitment, and decentralization. It is full of grace, truth, and wisdom, all the while keeping Jesus right at the center of everything. I dare say it may even help to soften the crusty interior of those of us who have spent more than a few years serving in the context of theological education for the church."

Miles V. Van Pelt, Alan Belcher Professor of Old Testament and Biblical Languages; Director, Summer Institute for Biblical Languages, Reformed Theological Seminary, Jackson, Mississippi

"I am exceedingly grateful to David Mathis and Jonathan Parnell for writing this helpful book. They touch on an issue of great concern in theological education, and on a topic of great concern to me personally. So much so, I wish that every seminary student in every seminary in America would read this insightful book and apply its teachings to their lives."

Jason K. Allen, President, Midwestern Baptist Theological
Seminary and College

"This is a book I have composed in my head many times, but never actually wrote down. Now I discover David Mathis and Jonathan Parnell actually wrote it down, and did a better job than I would have done. It is a guide to not only survive but to thrive in seminary (or any college or graduate program where you study theology)."

Don Sweeting, President, Reformed Theological Seminary,
Orlando

"Seminary students are called to live all of life before the face of God with application to their lives and future ministries. This devotional way of living means drinking deeply of both gospel grace and gospel truth with humble awareness of their dependence on the Holy Spirit inside and outside of the classroom. I highly commend this insightful book as must reading for present and prospective seminary students to gain this biblical perspective on seminary training. I would encourage seminary students everywhere to re-read this book at the beginning of each semester and pray that God would use this resource to help them take hold of Christ and his heart for their seminary experience."

Mark Dalbey, President and Assistant Professor of Practical
Theology, Covenant Theological Seminary

HOW TO

- STAY -

CHRISTIAN

- IN -

SEMINARY

DAVID MATHIS &
JONATHAN PARNELL

FOREWORD BY JOHN PIPER

WHEATON, ILLINOIS

How to Stay Christian in Seminary

Copyright © 2014 by David Mathis and Jonathan Parnell

Published by Crossway
   1300 Crescent Street
   Wheaton, Illinois 60187

Cover design: Tyler Deeb, Pedale Design

First printing 2014

Printed in the United States of America

Scripture quotations are from the ESV® Bible (*The Holy Bible, English Standard Version®*), copyright © 2001 by Crossway. 2011 Text Edition. Used by permission. All rights reserved.

Trade paperback ISBN: 978-1-4335-4030-1
Mobipocket ISBN: 978-1-4335-4032-5
PDF ISBN: 978-1-4335-4031-8
ePub ISBN: 978-1-4335-4033-2

Library of Congress Cataloging-in-Publication Data
Mathis, David, 1980–
 How to stay Christian in seminary / David Mathis and Jonathan Parnell.
  pages cm.
 Includes bibliographical references and index.
 ISBN 978-1-4335-4030-1 (tp)
 1. Theology—Study and teaching. 2. Spiritual life—Christianity. I. Title.
BV4020.M36   2014
248.8'92—dc23   2013019479

Crossway is a publishing ministry of Good News Publishers.

CH   25 24 23 22 21 20 19 18 17 16 15

To Megan and Melissa

CONTENTS

FOREWORD

BY JOHN PIPER

This book is by two men who did stay Christian in seminary. Really did. I have taught them and worked beside them for years. I love them and their vision. They are lovers of Jesus, lovers of the Bible, lovers of the church, lovers of the lost, and lovers of their wives and children. They fought for passion in all their studies, and God has given them their heart's desire.

My experience in seminary was very different from the sad stories I hear. I loved it. I flourished. I exploded, in fact. I could not get enough. Pursuing the knowledge of God and his word was not boring or deadening. Knowing more did not mean loving less. Just the opposite. If the wood of theology was dry, it burned the better. More facts *about* God meant more flame *for* God. More propositions, more passion. More sight, more savoring. I am eager for you to have such an experience. I think this book will help.

If there is anything I could underline, it would be this: cry to God day and night that he would open your eyes to see wonderful things in his word (Ps. 119:18). In other words, seek to experience every hour of study as a supernatural event. Everyone knows study is natural. Unbelievers can do it. What makes the difference is whether you can say with Paul, "I worked harder than any of them, though it was not I, but the grace of God that is with me" (1 Cor. 15:10). You do work. But if you are crying out for him, God works. And his work is decisive. That makes all the difference.

And never forget the stunning fact that the Bible is the word of God. Peter says the *writers* were inspired (2 Pet. 1:21), and Paul says the very *writings* themselves are inspired (2 Tim. 3:16). Never, never, never stop being amazed that the Bible is the communication of the Creator of the universe. It tells us things we cannot know any other way. To study it and proclaim it is an unspeakable privilege. And best of all, it is through the word that God himself comes to us and shows himself to us (1 Sam. 3:21).

Give, give, give. Give out what you are learning. Nothing grows in the Dead Sea, at least partly because there's no outlet. As you are fed, give food. As you burn, give warmth. As you see, show. As you are filled, spill. Find a flock to nurture. If you're married, that may be your wife and children. It may be, as it was for me, seventh-grade boys, then ninth-grade boys, then young married couples. But don't do so much ministry that you compromise the preciousness of your focus on study. Seminary days are unique days. They will probably never come again.

Don't think of your seminary years as the time when you learn what you need to know for ministry. If you do that, you will spend the rest of your life blaming the seminary for what you didn't get. I get very tired of those complaints. I have never blamed my seminary for anything I had to learn later. Expect that you will leave seminary with much yet to learn. Seminary is a more focused extension of high school and college. The aim of such formal education is to fit you to learn for the next fifty years.

Get skills. Get habits of mind. Get roots. Get vision. Get a big picture. Dig wells. Find orchards. Lay claim to mines. But don't even begin to think you will graduate with what you need to know. The second day on the job you will be faced with something that baffles you. Don't blame the seminary. Don't blame anyone. It's the way it is. Get on your knees. Open your Bible. Call a veteran. Take a risk.

And in it all, expect to suffer. Through many tribulations we must enter the kingdom (Acts 14:22)—and the ministry. There are things you cannot know without suffering. God has special tutorials in tribulation for his shepherds. Do not begrudge the seminars of suffering. His aim is to make you, like Jesus, a sympathetic shepherd. It's scary. Paul prayed that he would share Christ's sufferings and become like him in his death (Phil. 3:10). God answered him. He was forsaken at his last trial (2 Tim. 4:16), and the Romans took him out. We are not playing games.

If I could do it all over, I would—in spite of all the tears. There were afternoons I put my elbows on my desk, face in my hands, and wept over the theological confusion in my head. I think that is the price of dismantling joy-defeating doctrines. It is ironic that so many tears should be shed on the way to the fullness of joy. But that's the way it is. Truth must make room for itself. And that may mean demolishing the mental tenements where you have lived comfortably for a long time.

I am excited for you. May the Lord give you a praying heart, a ravenous mind, and an unwavering focus on the Book. May he embed you in the church, multiply your skills, and make you humble and strong through suffering.

Jesus is the same yesterday, today, and forever. The love that took him to the cross is the same he has for you today. He has all authority over whatever happens. He promises to be with you to the end of the age (including graduation day). You will plant and you will water. But God will give the growth. Let him be God. Work with all your might. Then say, "It was not I but the grace of God that was with me." He will keep you for himself. We offer this book as one way he will do it.

INTRODUCTION

Seminary: Life or Death?

DAVID MATHIS AND JONATHAN PARNELL

Seminary is dangerous. Its gospel fragrance proves life-giving to many. But for others—far too many others—its aroma can lead to death (2 Cor. 2:15–16). Seminarians whose hearts grow cold and dull not only leave the ministry; many leave the faith, and show themselves to never have been truly saved (1 John 2:19). We're not playing games here.

And we're not just talking about liberal seminaries when we warn of this danger. Of course, it's perilous to have professors playing fast and loose with the biblical text and Christian theology. But even the best of evangelical, confessional seminaries can be spiritually dangerous places, not mainly because of the administrators at the top or the teachers at the front, but because of the sinners in the seats.

However well the seminary as an institution does in contending for the truth once delivered to the saints (Jude 3), it can't keep "evil" outside its walls. It's too late. Evil has already broken the seal and penetrated the fortress into your seminary experience. It came in with you. The deepest danger comes in your heart, whose condition carries more influence than the doctrinal fidelity of your school. It is your heart that is "deceitful above all things, and desperately sick" (Jer. 17:9).

Regardless of the theological pedigree of your handpicked

and respected seminary, you, the theological student, face danger.

BIG HEADS, LITTLE HEARTS?

We could flesh out this danger in many ways. For starters, there's Helmut Thielicke's angle in his 1962 classic, *A Little Exercise for Young Theologians*. Simply put, students' heads often pick up on theology faster than their hearts and lives.

Seminary is a special season of preparation when you are presented with a veritable buffet of information. It's typically good information, mind you, precious information. But just because you can pile heaps of tasty food on one plate doesn't mean you can swallow it down easily. And just because you can force it down doesn't mean it will be nourishing. If you stuff your head full of more than your heart can digest, you will not be well.

Thielicke says the fundamental problem for seminarians is that intellectual accessibility exceeds spiritual capacity. Capturing the plight of far too many students, he writes, "He has not yet come to that maturity which would permit him to absorb into his own life and reproduce out of the freshness of his own personal faith the things which he imagines intellectually and which are accessible to him through reflection."[1] In other words, *the seminarian can say a lot of things he can't live.*

What's at stake in this situation? The church is soon to suffer. Fathead theology students parachute into local churches, where they model an insidious detachment between truth and love. With a subtle attitude of "smarter than thou," this kind of

---

[1] Helmut Thielicke, *A Little Exercise for Young Theologians*, trans. Charles L. Taylor (Grand Rapids: Eerdmans, 1962), 12.

seminarian spews God-talk isolated from faith and acts more like a mercenary than a member of the body. He may actually resemble more the Serpent than the Servant. "Such a person nevertheless has not comprehended a penny's worth of what it means to live on the battlefield of the risen Lord."[2]

ERNEST CHRISTIAN, MEMORIZING PARADIGMS

D. A. Carson gives another angle on the danger in the introduction to his book *Exegetical Fallacies*, notorious among students and pastors for how skillfully it exposes our bad interpretations. Simply put, Carson says the necessity of distancing yourself from your subject of study can be perilous when you're studying the things you most deeply believe.

Names changed to protect the guilty, Carson tells the story of "Ernest Christian," who was converted as a senior in high school, grew by leaps and bounds through a campus ministry while in college, sensed a call to full-time ministry, was affirmed by his local congregation, and "headed off to seminary with all the earnestness of a new recruit."

But at seminary, the story followed a path all too familiar to many of us:

After Ernest has been six months in seminary, the picture is very different. Ernest is spending many hours a day memorizing Greek morphology and learning the details of the itinerary of Paul's second missionary journey. Ernest has also begun to write exegetical papers; but by the time he has finished his lexical study, his syntactical diagram, his survey of critical

---

[2] Ibid., 29.

opinions, and his evaluation of conflicting evidence, somehow the Bible does not feel as alive to him as it once did. Ernest is troubled by this; he finds it more difficult to pray and witness than he did before he came to seminary.[3]

Carson goes on to explain how a good seminary must teach its students to distance their subjective thinking from the more objective meaning of the biblical text so that they might be shaped by the Scriptures rather than impose their own notions on the text. Such a learning process "is difficult, and can be costly." But it need not prove destructive, even if "some steps along the way are dangerous."[4]

Carson's exhortation is that students "work hard at integrating your entire Christian walk and commitment." Don't partition your devotional life from your academic pursuits. Instead, approach your studies devotionally. Be intentional to keep your mind and heart together rather than allowing them to be separated. Carson concludes with this warning: "Fail to work hard at such integration and you invite spiritual shipwreck."[5]

A TRIAL OF FAITH

Theologian and longtime professor John Frame also warns about the danger. In an article titled "Learning at Jesus' Feet: A Case for Seminary Training," Frame addresses seven objections, framed as questions, often raised against seminary. The second is, *Could seminary be a spiritual danger to me?* "This objection is not as strange as it may sound at first hearing," says Frame. "For some, seminary can be a trial of faith. One can become so

---

[3] D. A. Carson, *Exegetical Fallacies* (Grand Rapids: Baker Academic, 1996), 23.
[4] Ibid., 24.
[5] Ibid.

immersed in academic assignments, papers, technical terminology, Hebrew paradigms and such that he comes to feel far from God."[6]

So seminary can be dangerous. But neither Frame, Carson, Thielicke, nor we think this should keep you from it. Frame continues:

> Seminary does require a devotional discipline to match our academic discipline, but that challenge, on the whole, is a good thing. And what most students find is that once we face that challenge, the academic and the devotional merge in a wonderful way. The dry periods tend to be at the beginning, when you are struggling to master the basics. But when the theology of the Bible starts to come together in your mind, when you start to see the overall shape of it, your academic study will feed your soul.[7]

DON'T BE DETERRED

So, in penning this short book, we don't aim to deter you from seminary. We both have been beneficiaries of deeply enriching seminary experiences. Our desire is to help you be aware of the danger and appropriately sobered by it. We want you to face the challenge in earnest and see your faith strengthened, deepened, enlivened, and enriched by seminary, not shipwrecked.

Our hope is not to steer Christians away from seminaries, but to help those studying at seminary, or preparing to do so, in their expectations and approach to this season of life. If anything, we think, with Frame, "it would be a great benefit to

---

[6] John Frame, "Learning at Jesus' Feet: A Case for Seminary Training." Accessed online at http://www.frame-poythress.org/frame_articles/2003Learning.htm.
[7] Ibid.

the church, and to the lost, if many more Christians attended good seminaries. That would do much to reduce the appalling ignorance and immaturity in many Christian circles, which brings such discredit on the name of Christ."[8]

KEEPING THE HEART

Back to your heart. The heart is, after all, the "noble faculty of the soul," as the old Puritan John Flavel says in his little 1668 book, now titled *Keeping the Heart*.[9] Most generally, the heart refers to the inner man, and most importantly, a person's everlasting state depends upon its condition. Therefore, the "one great business of a Christian's life," claims Flavel, is to do heart-work, which he later explains as preserving the soul from sin and maintaining sweet communion with God.[10] And if this is true for the Christian life as a whole, it is just as true for the Christian in the season of theological training. We have some heart-work to do in the pages ahead.

In *How to Stay Christian in Seminary*, we're hoping, God helping us, to do precisely that—to help you stay Christian as you train for Christian ministry. We want to help you "keep the heart"—and to develop the heart from which you'll minister. We have seven ways in mind, each an outworking of the basic premise that what believers learn about God must affect the way they live. Put most plainly, we believe the key is intimacy with Jesus within a gospel-shaped community.

Chapter 1 is about what it's all about—the glory of God.

---

[8] Ibid.

[9] John Flavel, *Keeping the Heart: How to Maintain Your Love for God* (1668; repr., Ross-shire, Great Britain: Christian Focus, 2012), 14.

[10] Ibid., 16.

Chapter 2 addresses why and how you should be in awe at God's grace to you in Christ. Chapters 3 and 4 tackle Bible reading and prayer, those important personal means of grace. Chapter 5 envisions a faithful manner of study and ministry, reminding you that equipping doesn't mean getting strong. Chapter 6 focuses on the priority of the family. Chapter 7 is an appropriate grand finale as we celebrate the supremacy of Jesus toward which everything is trending. Lastly, steadying the whole project, the conclusion wraps it up by getting at why *today* matters.

Our prayer is that serious students of the Bible not only will avoid spiritual shipwreck but also will thrive in the disciplined study of the Scriptures, making the most of theological education now for the good of the church tomorrow and for the joy of their souls forever.

KNOW YOUR VALUE
OF VALUES

JONATHAN PARNELL

Jesus saved me. It really is amazing, though the story is simple.

I grew up in church, walked an aisle when I was eight, reprayed "the prayer" when I was fifteen, wandered when I got my driver's license, and was finally awakened after surviving a car wreck my senior year. Soon I found myself asking big questions: "Why am I alive? What am I supposed to do?" During my first semester of college, one thing became clear: I wanted to teach the Bible. And so began formal theological training.

It started with a holy, even jolly, ambition. I wanted to learn as much about Jesus as I could and then show him to others. What fueled my pursuit of ministry and the training involved was not how much I already knew but how much I already loved. Jesus had saved me, remember. He had *saved* me. I knew that, and I wanted more.

There are some things it is good to figure out before you start seminary. Sure, there's a lot to learn, and you must come with humility. But if you don't drop the anchor early, the calmest of seas will make you drift. Call it conviction, resolve, or whatever, but the first question to answer in seminary is why you're there. Why are you doing this? What is your rallying cry? What is the heart that pumps life into all your studies and ministry dreams?

LOOKING FOR STEEL

You can easily characterize the season of training by all the things you don't know. The conversations become fairly common. One classmate asks another about future plans. The answer is nothing certain. The second classmate then turns the question around and the dialogue stays squishy. No one really knows where he'll be after graduation. Even the tidiest of plans can fall through. Some theological commitments will be intensified; others will be recalibrated to a proper balance. It doesn't take long to see that you are surrounded by open-endedness. The seminary experience starts to feel like you're leaning on stained-glass windows when you need to be standing on brazen steel—the kind of steel that doesn't move.

On top of the uncertainty, the knowledge you are acquiring has a sneaky undercurrent. Before long, it subtly starts to pull. The more of it you get, the easier it becomes to slip into a mode of life that assumes accumulated information equals gospel maturity. This is what Paul Tripp calls "academizing our faith."[1] No one does this on purpose. It's like setting out with the good intention of building a bonfire but ending up with a mountain of sticks and no flame. The pile of wood may look impressive, but it fails to serve its function. It misses the point. Likewise, unless your resolve is as solid as steel, the stress of gained knowledge morphs and manipulates (if not shatters) the locus of our learning.

---

[1] Paul Tripp, *Dangerous Calling* (Wheaton, IL: Crossway, 2012), 42.

So, amid all the unknowns and the dangers of increased knowing, it is crucial to know this: *your value of values.*

Be clear on what you care about the most, which, if we're faithful to the Bible, is not a multiple-choice question. The great foundation and goal of the universe is the glory of God. The foundation and goal of your studies and ministry should be no different. More than anything else, energized by grace, you want our triune God to be high and lifted up. You treasure him. You delight in him. You hallow his name. You are committed to his fame and renown. *You are about the glory of God.*

But what does that mean? What is the glory of God? And how can you make it the foundation and goal of your seminary years? There are two more steps on the way out of this chapter. First, I want to define the glory of God, and second, I want to suggest a practical way to integrate this chief value into the details of your training.

THE GLORY OF GOD DEFINED

What is the glory of God? What is it that Moses asked to see in Exodus 33:18? What is it that John 1:14 declares the apostles saw in Jesus?

Consider that holy exchange between Moses and God in Exodus 33. We see that Moses's request to see God's glory follows a previous request: "Please show me now your ways, that I may know you in order to find favor in your sight" (v. 13). Though he says it in different ways, in both instances Moses is asking to behold the same thing. When he asks to see God's ways, he asks for something that can be shown—God's glory.

The apostle John affirms this same concept in the opening of his Gospel account. The glory of God is indeed something seen. John declares that the apostles saw the glory of God in the person of his Son. Jesus came to embody and display the ways of God, and to that end, he was full of grace and truth (John 1:14).

For starters, then, we learn that the glory of God is not a distant attribute. Neither is it some abstract description of God's mysterious wonders. Rather, the glory of God is a showcase. It is, by its very nature, something revealed. It is a manifestation. For God to glorify himself is for him to communicate who he is. As Jonathan Edwards writes, "God glorifies himself in communicating himself, and he communicates himself in glorifying himself."[2]

God hears Moses and answers, "I will make all my goodness pass before you and will proclaim before you my name 'The LORD'" (Ex. 33:19). The glory of the Lord is to "pass by" Moses (v. 22), which it soon does:

> The LORD descended in the cloud and stood with him there, and proclaimed the name of the LORD. The LORD passed before him and proclaimed, "The LORD, the LORD, a God merciful and gracious, slow to anger, and abounding in steadfast love and faithfulness, keeping steadfast love for thousands, forgiving iniquity and transgression and sin, but who will by no means clear the guilty, visiting the iniquity of the fathers on the children and the children's children, to the third and the fourth generation." (34:5–7)

---

[2] Jonathan Edwards, "Approaching the End of God's Grand Design," in *Sermons and Discourses, 1743–1758*, vol. 25 of *The Works of Jonathan Edwards*, ed. Wilson H. Kimnach (New Haven, CT: Yale University Press, 2006), 117.

So the glory of God is something seen—revealed—and something proclaimed. Answering Moses's prayer, God descended and proclaimed his name. For God to proclaim his name is another way of saying God showcases his ways. God's name is his "enacted identity."[3] It is the banner of how God acts based upon who he is, full of grace and truth.

Make no mistake, God is utterly incomparable and eternally inexhaustible. Only he knows himself fully. But he has told us something about himself. He has told us his name, revealing that he is a certain kind of God who acts in certain ways. God's glory, then, is the picture he gives of who he is, seen preeminently in the person of Jesus. God's glory is the proclamation of his name, the shining forth of his ways.

Therefore, for us to say that we are about the glory of God means that we are about God being seen for who he is. The steel foundation and center for our learning is that God would be known as God through our lives. The anchor that can keep our hearts steady amid all the studying is the resolve that Jesus must be tasted and treasured by us and through us.

DOWN IN THE DETAILS

But merely having this resolve isn't enough. We need to make it stick. Alongside the miraculous grace of God in Jesus, I have in mind one practical way to do so: a mission statement (or something like it). You need a clear, concise statement that you can easily remember and quickly return to—something in which you say what it's all about, in which you declare the most important value among all your other values.

---

[3] John Webster, *Holiness* (Grand Rapids: Eerdmans, 2003), 36.

This idea came from a friend about six years ago. My wife and I were newly married and already on the brink of making some big life decisions. We were contemplating the prospect of relocating our fledgling family to a place with a winter climate we couldn't fathom, people we didn't know, and a job that didn't exist so I could complete a degree program for which I didn't feel qualified. It was the front end of seminary in Minneapolis. After I expressed some of my anxiety to my friend, he asked me, "So, what's your family's mission statement?" I'm pretty sure there was a stutter or silence, perhaps a nod. His question was more of a suggestion, the kind that draws you in. I didn't have a mission statement, but I knew then that I needed one.

Basically, a mission statement for seminary is the articulation of what you value the most. Consider good institutions. Step one for a faithful institution is to know what it is about. That mission is articulated in a memorable line that becomes the point of gravity around which everything operates. Markets change, technology matures, but the mission stays the course. The institution either withstands the tide of change or goes out of business. The better folks in the organization know and believe the mission, the better chance the organization has to succeed. Everyone is working toward the same thing, aiming their individual 9-to-5 days at that chief goal.

As part of a content team at desiringGod.org, I recently visited the Facebook offices in New York. I don't remember the exact slogans, but Facebook has stuff written across the entirety of its office walls in big block letters. This technique is motivational and has a trendy feel, but it is also brilliant. The idea is to keep the mission explicit and keep the staff conscious of it.

Facebook employees do different tasks, but the words on the walls remind them why it all happens.

It can be like that for you, the seminarian, except that your classes are the employees. First, carefully craft your mission statement. It can be your own biblically informed words or actual phrases from biblical texts. Make it a clear but rich sentence that encapsulates your desire for Jesus to be treasured in and through your life. The goal is to help you crystallize your mission in your mind and heart, giving you something you can come back to again and again.

Once you have it down, write it all over your walls (figuratively). Hold it up as you browse the academic catalog. Inscribe it inside the front covers of your textbooks. Make all of your classes go to work for you, each one aiming at your one great goal. And when the assignments feel unbearable and the clouds of discouragement set in, hold up that mission statement. Remember what you're in this for.

You are about the glory of God. You exist for Jesus Christ to be displayed and delighted in through your life, and don't you forget it. Know your value of values.

BE FASCINATED
WITH GRACE

DAVID MATHIS

We're all too prone to take God's grace for granted. Perhaps Bible students are especially likely to do so as they perceive themselves to be climbing the ladder of formal theological training.

At the heart of the danger of seminary is coming to treat the grace of God lightly. But a healthy experience of seminary drives you to do precisely the opposite.

THE CENTRALITY OF GRACE

Grace is no peripheral thing in Christianity. God's astoundingly lavish favor toward us terribly undeserving sinners, because of Jesus, is at the very center of our faith. If seminarians lose their taste for grace, they have no good business calling themselves Christians, much less putting themselves forward as leaders in the church.

But here's the catch: you can't just make yourself stay soft to grace. Or can you?

Ultimately, it is only by more of God's grace that we sinners stay fascinated with his lavish grace to us. But there are "means of grace" that God is pleased to use in keeping his people keen on grace, and we'll address these in the chapters to come. As you study, you need to avail yourself of these means, and do so with a regular, conscious plea—something like this: "God, keep me warm to your grace. Help me to be endlessly astounded that in Jesus you've shown such amazing favor to such an undeserving rebel as me."

GRACE AND THE GOSPEL

As you explicitly ask God to keep you fascinated with his grace, the first means you should employ is this: relentlessly keep the gospel central.

The gospel of Jesus is the epicenter of Christian grace, and true Christian grace is ever shaped by the message of the Messiah crucified for sinners. Ask how each seminary class and each assigned book relates to Jesus and his good news for sinners. Look for Jesus in all the Scriptures (more on this in chapter 7). Watch for God's costly grace in every book of the Bible. Seminary is a good opportunity to go deep with the grace of God in the gospel.

BEING REAL WITH OUR SIN

Going deep with grace includes not being afraid to know yourself as deeply sinful. Keeping the gospel close frees you to look honestly at your sins, showing you all the more the wonder of the grace you have received.

Don't be afraid to linger over passages such as Ephesians 2:1–3 and identify deeply with sinners. But don't think mainly of others; know that you yourself were once "dead in the trespasses and sins" (v. 1). Even if you've been a believer as long as you can remember, there's still plenty of remaining sin in you, enough for you to know its insidiousness and what trajectory it will lead you on if it is unrestrained. Every believer knows all too well "the spirit that is now at work in the sons of disobedience" (v. 2). There is some sense in which it still courses through each Christian's veins, even with the gracious pumping of a new heart.

Let's admit it, we believers know "the passions of our flesh." They are in us—evidence that we "were by nature children of wrath, like the rest of mankind" (v. 3). The omnipotent wrath of God once was justly over us. Apart from Jesus, and God's extraordinary grace, it would still be over us.

THE FLOOD OF GOD'S GRACE

Spend a few moments trying to breathe the suffocating air of sin and its just penalty, then feel the flood of grace in passages such as Ephesians 2:4–7. Despite human beings' dastardly rebellion and vacuous spiritual poverty, "God, being rich in mercy, because of the great love with which he loved us, even when we were dead in our trespasses, made us alive together with Christ—by grace you have been saved—and raised us up with him and seated us with him in the heavenly places in Christ Jesus, so that in the coming ages he might show the immeasurable riches of his grace in kindness toward us in Christ Jesus."

Grace: despite our rebellion, covering our past, flooding our present, and increasing forever into the future. May God never let you cool to his grace. Even (and especially) in seminary, may you never cease seeking to "continue in the grace of God" (Acts 13:43).

NEVER TAKE GRACE FOR GRANTED

For Christians, boasting is excluded, both in our salvation and in everything we do—seminary work included: "What do you have that you did not receive? If then you received it, why do you boast as if you did not receive it?" (1 Cor. 4:7).

Don't be under the delusion that seminary automatically makes you grow in grace (2 Pet. 3:18). In fact, it can have quite the opposite effect. Beware lest frequent handling of holy things, such as the Scriptures, good doctrine, and the gospel itself, causes you to lose your wonder about them. And especially don't be flippant with grace. For God's sake, your own sake, and the sake of the people you'll one day serve, never take grace for granted.

STUDY THE WORD FOR MORE THAN WORDS

DAVID MATHIS

Learn a lesson from Jerry Seinfeld: *daily Bible intake is about soul survival.*

When his wildly successful sitcom ended, Seinfeld went on a nationwide stand-up comedy tour called "I'm Telling You for the Last Time." The routine was recorded for compact disc (remember those?) at New York's Broadhurst Theater in August 1998. At the end is a question-and-answer segment, during which a zealous fan shouts, "Do you have a favorite *Seinfeld* episode?"

Seinfeld answers:

> I get this question quite often. I don't really have a favorite; they're all kind of my babies. I did the best I could with each one. [*Audience applauds*.]
>
> You know, comedy is kind of a survival industry. Comedians are very much into just surviving. It's like if I were to ask you, "What is your favorite breath of air that you've ever taken?" You would say, "Whichever one I'm taking that gets me to the next one." That's kind of the mindset.

That kind of mind-set is a wise one for the seminary student (indeed, every Christian) to embrace. You won't appreciate the fact that you took a deep breath an hour ago unless you're still breathing now. A great meal you ate a month ago won't do you much good if you haven't eaten since. Likewise, delighting in God through taking in his word isn't an annual, monthly, or even weekly event for the healthy Christian, but a daily rhythm.

KEEPING YOUR SOUL ALIVE

There is more to seminary, and the whole of the Christian life, than the necessity of pursuing daily soul survival in the Scriptures, but this need must not be overlooked. An otherwise impressive theology degree is utterly unimpressive if your soul has shriveled in the course of study.

As Christians, daily Bible intake is to our souls what breathing, eating, and drinking are to our physical bodies. As the incarnate Word himself says, quoting Deuteronomy 8:3, "Man shall not live by bread alone, but by every word that comes from the mouth of God" (Matt. 4:4). Our souls will die without the word of God. So, like Seinfeld says about comedians, seminarians should be "very much into just surviving"—at least in this sense.

MAKE YOUR STUDIES DEVOTIONAL

First, seek to make your seminary studies devotional. Pray for God's help before class, before studying, before writing a paper or taking a test, and during all these activities. Continually consecrate your studies to Jesus and ask him to freshly meet you in them, keep your spiritual blood flowing, and keep you soft to his grace.

It is important for every Christian, and perhaps especially

for seminary students, to never come to the Scriptures with anything less than a devotional approach. Whatever the assignment, intentionally seek the growth and warming of your soul. There's no spiritually neutral gear when handling the Bible. You don't need to learn the lesson far too many have experienced about trifling with holy things—you either survive or shrivel.

KEEP SPACE FOR DAILY DEVOTIONS

Second, set aside at least a brief season daily to focus on feeding your soul. Find a good patch in the Scriptures (maybe through an annual Bible-reading plan), one you're not studying in preparation for a class, a test, or a sermon, and graze a while, just for your spiritual well-being. Crumbs from such a meal will inevitably bless those to whom you minister, but try not to make your future flock (or present ministry) your explicit focus in this feeding. The aim is the daily strengthening and sustaining of your soul.

An often-helpful reminder to seminary students is to not read merely for information. Such information, glorious as it is, won't keep your heart soft and your soul breathing. What we desperately need is spiritual sight of the living Christ. We need the person of Jesus himself, whom we find in and through the Scriptures. Our souls long for a living connection with the living God-man. We were made for this.

Therefore, be on the unashamed lookout for Jesus and his gospel, for soul-satisfaction that runs up verses and doctrines to a person, the God-man, rather than terminating on concepts and ideas. In an explicitly "devotional" time, set out to explicitly enjoy Jesus in the Scriptures as your great end, not as a means to anything else, whether it is a class assignment or ministering to others in some way.

READING SCRIPTURE THROUGH THE RIGHT GRID

John 5 shows the folly of fixing on the Scriptures while ignoring the God of grace. Jesus crossed paths with a troop who liked to think of themselves as soaked in the Scriptures, but they were getting them all wrong, taking them in through the wrong grid. What an epic tragedy: they had God himself in the flesh, standing in their very midst, and they missed him because their Bible reading was going awry with self at the center. Jesus said to them, "You search the Scriptures because you think that in them you have eternal life; and it is they that bear witness about me, yet you refuse to come to me that you may have life" (John 5:39–40).

The lesson for us is to never disconnect our searching of the Scriptures from a conscious awareness and pursuit of Jesus as our Savior, Lord, and Treasure. The gospel of Jesus is the core, culmination, and meaning of the Scriptures. No matter how passionate the study, regular Bible intake that is not in accord with the truth of the gospel is akin, at best, to zeal without knowledge (Rom. 10:2).

Displace the gospel from the center, and studiousness in the Scriptures soon becomes a massive self-salvation project.

BIBLE INTAKE AND PREACHING TO YOURSELF

As you keep the gospel in view, don't miss this: God does not intend for the message of the gospel to be cut loose from the Scriptures. Regular Bible intake—whether it's reviewing memorized Scripture passages, enjoying Bible-infused conversations with fellow believers, or receiving the public preaching of God's word—serves to shape, strengthen, and sustain your daily preaching of the gospel to yourself. The Scriptures, rightly understood with Jesus at the center, nourish your heart and sharpen your mind, so that you are able to rehearse the truth of the gospel with texture, edge, and definition, with freshness and power.

The message of the gospel is not meant to be something you "get," carve into canned lines, and tell yourself over and over for a lifetime as some sort of magic mantra to fight sin. God means for you to be regularly pushed and formed, hurt and healed, challenged and encouraged by passages you've never heard before, haven't given enough attention to, or haven't considered in a while. He means for you to understand even your best-known verses at new depths, and know the power of his grace more deeply, through new applications, as you encounter situations in life you've never faced before.

THE SHELF LIFE ON PREACHING THE GOSPEL TO YOURSELF

One last caution: if you're faithfully "preaching the gospel" to your soul day in and day out but distancing yourself from regular Bible intake, your "freshness" is fading. There's an expiration date on the fruit of preaching to yourself once it's off the vine.

Don't think I'm down on preaching the gospel to oneself. I love it. I commend it. It's one of my main conscious sources for sanctification, an indispensable weapon for fighting the fight of faith. I eat this fruit daily. I warn you about the "shelf life" on gospel self-preaching in the hope that you will guard and preserve this precious reality in your Christian life.

My concern is that those who are convinced of their ongoing need for the gospel should take care that their so-called gospel-centeredness does not lead to laxity with the Scriptures. God has designed the two to be united. And what God has joined together, let no man separate.

Without relentlessly reorienting yourself to the gospel, your study of the Scriptures quickly veers off course. And without keeping yourself freshly filled with the Scriptures, your gospel self-preaching soon runs on empty.

KEEPING YOUR GOSPEL FRESH

This is why God gives us teachers, fellow believers, and access to his objective "external word," as Martin Luther called it, amazingly preserved in a book for millennia, to continue shaping and upholding the church today. He means for us regularly to hear other Christians articulate the truths most precious, and to be pressed time and again with God's own inerrant speaking in human language in the biblical canon.

So keep the gospel central in your sanctification and keep it ever in view in your Bible reading and study. Eat daily the fruit of preaching the gospel to yourself. And keep your stock fresh with regular picking from the cornucopia of Bible intake in its varied forms.

You can never afford to settle for anything less than the words of the Bible, but extreme as it may seem, your soul needs *more than words*, more than facts, more than studies and new head knowledge. You need the Word himself. Your soul needs Jesus to survive. And for now, the devotional imbibing of the Scriptures is an essential way to find him.

PUSH YOUR BOOKS
ASIDE AND PRAY

JONATHAN PARNELL

Imagine a desk that is cluttered with stacks of books and photocopied journal articles. Your big paper deadline is coming up, and it's time to get to work.

But that's not the main reason you pull out the chair and sit down before such a scene. Fulfilling that assignment isn't the primary aim in opening those books and thumbing through those articles. Your chief goal is to encounter God. That's what it means for study to be devotional, as David explained in the previous chapter.

B. B. Warfield says the same in his essay "The Religious Life of Theological Students." But while affirming that theological studies are "religious exercises of the most rewarding kind," Warfield doesn't stop here. He goes on to say that there are other religious exercises that demand your "punctual attention." Though study should be devotional, study is not the extent of your devotional life. There are other aspects that cannot be neglected "without the gravest damage" to your soul.[1]

---

[1] Benjamin B. Warfield, "The Religious Life of Theological Students," *The Master's Seminary Journal* 6/2 (Fall 1995), 187. Accessed online at http://www.tms.edu/tmsj/tmsj6g.pdf.

If you were to throw all the aspects of your devotional life into a hat and draw one, there is no doubt that good arguments could be made for why that aspect is a non-negotiable. Fair enough. But we won't be able to cover them all in this little book. Time forces us to perform triage, and for now the subject is prayer. Prayer warrants a particular emphasis, and I am eager to bring it up, not because I'm great at it, but because of how it gets at the heart of all your study.

However, before we get into the subject of prayer full-throttle, there are a few preliminary points to make.

THE WONDER OF GOD'S REVELATION

Study is a good place to start. First, you study a lot as a seminarian. Second, study necessitates wonder. Think about it: study is what we Christians do with a body of knowledge. And we can study God only because he has established a body of knowledge about himself. *God has made himself known.*

Don't skim over that truth. With so many commentaries, articles, textbooks, lectures, and assignments, not to mention blog posts and gospel tweets, available to us, we can easily become numb to the fact that we are able to know anything about God. All this information, all the effortless access to truth about God, freezes over our sense of miracle. We then presume. We read ourselves into a sense of entitlement, as if the availability of all this knowledge makes perfectly good sense and we have a right to it.

This is where the book of Job helps us. Have you seen the God of those pages? When we start reading this book, we instantly realize our privileged perspective as the audience. The book is dramatic irony at its best. We get to read the dialogue between God and Satan. We know more than Job does about why he suffers. We get to hear his friends' advice, along with Job's response to each. Then we meet Elihu, the "only person with both an Israelite name and Israelite genealogy" (Job 32:2).[2] He extols God's greatness and witnesses to his might. Like a helicopter tour over the Grand Canyon, his act is short but enough to boggle your mind. As Elihu speaks to Job, he speaks to us:

> Behold, God is exalted in his power; who is a teacher like him? Who has prescribed for him his way, or who can say, "You have done wrong"? Remember to extol his work, of which men have sung. All mankind has looked on it; man beholds it from afar. (Job 36:22–25)

Then he adds:

> Behold, God is great, and we know him not; the number of his years is unsearchable. (v. 26)

The book of Job has much to say about God, and here—in the definitive testimony to who God is up to this point of the story—is a confession of God's incomprehensibility: "*God is great, and we know him not.*" God is inexhaustible, with no beginning and no end. He has no border to his magnitude and no cap to his power. Really, we cannot dream how amazing he is.

This truth matters especially for seminarians because I fear many imagine God as far too small. Even if you say the right words and articulate good doctrine, if you are not somehow unsettled by God's mystery, somehow overcome by his

---

[2] Stephen Dempster, *Dominion and Dynasty: A Biblical Theology of the Hebrew Bible*, New Studies in Biblical Theology, ed. D. A. Carson (Downers Grove, IL: InterVarsity, 2003), 204.

greatness, it's probably because you have domesticated him. Accessibility to information about him has inoculated you to his grandeur.

But remember, please, how incomparable he is. God is the one who is greater than that which can be fathomed. Just stretch your imagination. Go as far as you can, and then a little further. You're still not even close. The capacity of the human intellect is as nothing to his volume. As Herman Bavinck says, "He infinitely transcends our picture of him, our ideas of him, our language concerning him."[3] You will never wrap your head around him. That's what it means for God to be God. Only he knows himself fully.

But all that I'm saying here about what we can't know is *something we do know*. Stay with me. The very fact that we know that God is incomprehensible is itself an evidence of what he has graciously let us comprehend. That we have any picture of him—or any idea or any language—is a wonder. It would never be the case had not God bent down on his knees, as it were, and spoken to us as we do to babies.[4] Though he is incomprehensible, God has revealed something about himself to his finite creatures. Though only he knows himself fully, God has leaned over for us and has come down to us to give us truth about who he is—truth that we can trust and on which we can bank our lives.

---

[3] Herman Bavinck, *Reformed Dogmatics*, vol. 2, *God and Creation*, ed. John Bolt, trans. John Vriend (Grand Rapids: Baker, 2004), 47.

[4] John Calvin writes: "For who even of slight intelligence does not understand that, as nurses commonly do with infants, God is wont in a measure to 'lisp' in speaking to us? Thus such forms of speaking do not so much express clearly what God is like as accommodate the knowledge of him to our slight capacity. To do this he must descend far beneath his loftiness." (*Institutes of the Christian Religion*, ed. John T. McNeill, trans. Ford Lewis Battles, Library of Christian Classics vols. 20–21 [Louisville, KY: Westminster John Knox, 1960], 1.13.1).

REVELATION FOR FELLOWSHIP

Now prayer is in our sights. But there's one more preliminary point. As stunning as it is that the incomprehensible God has made himself known to us, God is not content that we look upon his truth from a distance. We may step back for a moment and consider it in awe, but we can't do this for long. The purpose of God's revelation is not that we stand over it and observe, but that we be drawn in and enjoy *him*. The goal of revelation is fellowship.

Here's what God says to us in 1 John 1:1–2:

> That which was from the beginning, which we have heard, which we have seen with our eyes, which we looked upon and have touched with our hands, concerning the word of life—the life was made manifest, and we have seen it, and testify to it and proclaim to you the eternal life, which was with the Father and was made manifest to us.

Notice how the apostle John begins his first letter. He talks about revelation, and Jesus is the subject. We apostles heard him and saw him, John explains. We even touched him, this "word of life," whom we now "proclaim to you." The Father has made Jesus manifest, and John is writing this epistle to bear testimony. That is to say, Jesus *is* the revelation of God. Those who have seen Jesus have seen the Father (John 14:9). Jesus has made him known (John 1:18). Period. No qualifications. The Father has spoken to us through him (Heb. 1:2).

Said another way, Jesus is the very word of the Father. And this word, Jesus, is both revelatory and redemptive. John proclaims Jesus not so that we may merely learn things about God, but that we might have fellowship with him (1 John 1:3). Jesus is God's call to fellowship (1 Cor. 1:9); to receive him is to become God's child (John 1:12–13). God makes himself known to us so that we will *know him*—that we'll know him through the Son and by the Spirit, and that we'll be glad in all that he is for us as *our* God.

Understanding this fills out the meaning of revelation. The point is that God doesn't just show to show; he shows for a purpose. And the purpose is his people's joy in him. God gives a view of his glory—the display of who he is—to effect something in us, namely, value, esteem, love, and delight for and in him.[5] This is the life of fellowship with God—the fellowship to which God draws us by shining forth his glory. When we see him and know him, we are not made his children begrudgingly, nor can we dispassionately observe who he is for us. As his knowledge shines forth, we receive it by faith—satisfied in him and in the depths of his majesty. It's not about ideas alone. God, the very God, has come near, and more than near. Indeed, our fellowship is with the Father and with his Son Jesus Christ (1 John 1:3).

THE TONIC OF PRAYER

Revelation, chock-full of wonder, is meant for fellowship. I have been arcing toward the subject of prayer throughout this chapter, and now we've finally arrived. But what's up with all these preliminary points? What do revelation and fellowship have to do with prayer?

---

[5] Jonathan Edwards writes, "As it is a thing valuable and desirable in itself that God's glory should be seen and known, so when known, it seems equally reasonable and fit, it should be valued and esteemed, loved and delighted in, answerably to its dignity." ("Dissertation I: Concerning the End for Which God Created the World," in *Ethical Writings*, vol. 8 of *The Works of Jonathan Edwards*, ed. Paul Ramsey. Accessed online at http://archive.is/IggL.

The answer is that prayer makes the most sense in this context. Prayer is our fitting response to God making himself known. Doxological and confessional, prayer is our participation in the fellowship God has accomplished. We can't begin praying without acknowledging God's greatness and his relationship to us. We may not speak of it, but true prayer must at least assume it. "Our Father in heaven, hallowed be your name," the Lord Jesus taught us to pray (Matt. 6:9). We recognize a God who is worthy for his glory to be displayed and treasured everywhere. And we recognize *this God* to be *our Father*—a Father whose Spirit bears witness with our spirits that we are his children (Rom. 8:16).

Prayer is where we agree with God that he is who he says he is and we are who he says we are. Kevin Vanhoozer writes, "Prayer, like doctrine itself, is a powerful tonic of reality."[6] Prayer is when we *snap out of it*—out of the busyness, out of our culture-imposed identities, out of the notion that studying theology is about mere information. Praying, you see, is the most real thing we do. It is tapping into a level of reality to which we have no right, but to which we have been graciously welcomed by the love of God in Christ. It is a reality in which, because of Jesus, we feel most at home. And it should be inconceivable that anyone could ever be God's student without it.

Now back to that scene of the cluttered desktop. Towers of books fill the space, sticky notes protruding from their pages. This is your study space, and you go there devotionally. As you breathe in each page or construct each sentence, your heart is

---

[6] Kevin J. Vanhoozer, *The Drama of Doctrine: A Canonical-Linguistic Approach to Christian Theology* (Louisville, KY: Westminster John Knox, 2005), 394.

inclined to God, or at least that's our hope. Indeed, in Warfield's words cited above, study is a "religious exercise of the most rewarding kind."

However, at some point, you must push your books aside. You must pause and pray, for only prayer can transform information into intimacy.

Bow your head and tell the Father all your heart. Thank him for the Bible. Cast on him all your anxieties, for he cares for you. Marvel before him that he knows every star and tends his flock like a shepherd. Be in wonder that he really did choose you in Christ before the foundation of the world. Be in awe at what happened the Friday Jerusalem fell dark. Be astounded by that moment the stone was rolled away and Jesus conquered death. Be stunned that God's triune glory will cover the earth as the waters cover the sea.

God has made himself known, and he has made himself known to you, drawing you into his fellowship. He is your God, your Father, Jesus your Savior, the Spirit your Comforter.

Push those books aside and pray.

LOVE THAT JESUS CALLS THE WEAK

JONATHAN PARNELL

We were all huddled around a circle of tables. Thursday noon meant "Table Talk" for the guys at Bethlehem Seminary, and on this particular day we were talking church unity with our pastor and school chancellor, John Piper. He had raised that subject to kick things off, though the conversation had morphed into a discussion on various denominations and influences within American evangelicalism. We were simply carrying the conversation along by our questions. Then Benjamin spoke up.

"Pastor John," he began, "as seminarians at Bethlehem, and since we have been deeply impacted by you, what do you want us to be like? What should characterize us?"

The room became instantly still. This was a really good question. We all leaned forward, waiting for Pastor John's reply. He looked down at his Bible, deep in thought.

"I want you to be more like John Newton than John Knox," he came back. "Knox was passionate and wild, even abrasive at times." We knew these could be good qualities (minus the abrasive part). But then Pastor John continued.

"But John Newton," he said, beaming with a smile, "Newton was glad he was saved!"

NEWTON KNEW WEAKNESS

Newton, the one-time slave-ship captain in eighteenth-century England, was wonderfully redeemed, and lived conscious of it. The gospel of Jesus crucified and risen broke into his dark heart and then shone brightly through it. After his conversion, over the course of some time, he went on to serve the church as an Anglican pastor and hymn writer, composing the most popular song in the world, "Amazing Grace."

But one of Newton's most fascinating characteristics is precisely what our pastor highlighted. Through all of Newton's subsequent success as a gospel minister, he never forgot what it meant to be lost and then found. He was tender to the story of God's mercy in his life. It was too wonderful for him to make a mere footnote.

I have the impression from learning about Newton that if you could go back in time and have a cup of coffee with him, you would be sure this man had tasted God's grace. I imagine that amazement radiated from him.

At the same time, Newton was extremely gifted. He was eccentric—a man who could talk shop with the roughest of sailors and compose a hymn gentle enough for a child to sing. But as gifted as he was, he was surrounded by men even more gifted—and he would have been the first to say it. For instance, one of his longtime friends was William Cowper, a preeminent poet with an impressive pedigree, whose literary skills are manifestly superior to Newton's in a book of hymns they wrote together.[1] Add to this his teamwork with Member of Parliament William Wilberforce in the abolition of the slave trade. Unlike the up-and-coming Wilberforce, Newton's role in the abolition was less political and more personal. He was a behind-the-scenes coach to Wilberforce and contributed best to the cause's success by confessing the atrocities he had seen and participated in.

Newton was remarkable in his own right, but the exceptional talent of his closest friends and colleagues kept him from thinking too highly of himself (Rom. 12:3). His influence grew wide and deep, but for him it all came back to grace—amazing grace. God had saved him. He was a miracle. He knew that whatever good would come from his life, it was because of God's greatness, not his. Newton understood that he was weak.

THE BEAUTY OF BEING WEAK

If we Christians were honest with ourselves, we'd think more like Newton. We would understand that we are weak.

We see weakness everywhere in the New Testament in several different forms. Jesus told his disciples that, in contrast to the spirit, the flesh is weak (Mark 14:38). Luke, in Paul's voice, refers to the weak as those who are economically disadvantaged (Acts 20:35). The book of Romans tells us that Jesus died for us while we were still *weak*, that is, while we were ungodly and lacked any possibility of deserving the slightest good (Rom. 5:8). But we are also weak when we pray, when we lack the words or know-how (Rom. 8:26). Then there are Christians who manifest

[1] Jonathan Aitken, *John Newton: From Disgrace to Amazing Grace* (Wheaton, IL: Crossway, 2007), 214ff.

weakness when they can't get past judging others on matters of conscience (Rom. 14:1–4). Also throw in this pile the physical infirmities that Paul seems to cite in 2 Corinthians 10:10, the thorn in the flesh in 2 Corinthians 12:7, and the litany of unpleasantness in 2 Corinthians 12:10. One way or another, we have heard the Bible speak about weakness.

The context, of course, determines the specific meaning of weakness, but every use is connected back to the general idea of deficiency. If there is one word that encapsulates this concept, it is *lack*. When it comes down to it, believers are like grass, passing shadows, or vapors in the wind (Ps. 103:15; 144:4; James 4:14).

Weakness means we don't have what it takes. It means we are not sovereign, omniscient, or invincible. We are not in control, we don't know everything, and we can be stopped. Weakness means that we desperately need God.

THE GOAL OF SEMINARY

"Consider your calling, brothers," the apostle Paul reminds all seminary students, "not many of you were wise according to worldly standards, not many were powerful, not many were of noble birth" (1 Cor. 1:26). Speaking in a social sense, Paul's "not many" phrase suggests that what he says doesn't apply to everyone, but it most likely includes you (it certainly includes me).

Most of you didn't come to faith in Jesus with the intellectual endorsement of secular scholars or the accolades of worldly fame. The truth is, you are weak all around. You are weak, plain and simple. But in your weakness, God has called you, and therefore you have entered seminary for theological training.

You go to seminary to grow, yes. You go to seminary to learn and steward your gifts, absolutely. But here's the thing: *the goal of seminary is not to become unweak.*

First Corinthians 1:26 can begin to make less sense to you, though. You breathe in dense theological truth, get your bearings in the original languages, consult high-level scholarship, and perhaps even sign up for a student membership in the Evangelical Theological Society, and somewhere along the way you mistake seminary to be not the place where you become equipped but where you become stronger. You think it's about bulking up.

It can happen in two ways. Either you don't feel very foolish in the way you're able to dissect Jonathan Edwards's "Essay on the Trinity" or you realize it's so far over your head that you grumble to God that he didn't give you a higher IQ. Both ways happen when you make seminary about strength. Both ways miss the holiness of your weakness.

WEAK MINISTER, STRONG MESSIAH

Whichever side you are tempted to fall toward, you must sink your cleats into the ground of God's calling. Here's 1 Corinthians 1:27–31:

> But God chose what is foolish in the world to shame the wise; God chose what is weak in the world to shame the strong; God chose what is low and despised in the world, even things that are not, to bring to nothing things that are, so that no human being might boast in the presence of God. And because of him you are in Christ Jesus, who became to us wisdom from God, righteousness and sanctification and redemption, so that, as it is written, "Let the one who boasts, boast in the Lord."

You must love that Jesus calls the weak.

I urge you to love the biblical narrative: how Abraham was "as good as dead" when he fathered Isaac (Heb. 11:12), how insignificant Judah should have been as Jacob's fourth son (Gen. 29:31–35), how Gideon needed reassurance after reassurance (Judg. 6:36–40), how David was the little one (1 Sam. 16:11). You should marvel that no matter how remarkable your giftings or how simple your understanding, the message you proclaim is sheer stupidity to the world. Intellectual proficiency takes a back seat when your only hope is in what some call offensive and others call folly. Therefore, determine to be known less for your strengths in academic rigor and more for how that rigor helps you grasp what it means that the God-man was crucified to save the world. Embrace your weakness. Bring it all back to grace.

In southern England, in a small, bustling town called Olney, outside the parish church of St. Peter and St. Paul, rests a cold gravestone of an old pastor. It reads:

JOHN NEWTON

ONCE AN INFIDEL AND LIBERTINE

A SERVANT OF SLAVES IN AFRICA

WAS

BY THE RICH MERCY OF OUR LORD AND SAVIOUR

JESUS CHRIST

PRESERVED, RESTORED, PARDONED

AND APPOINTED TO PREACH THE FAITH

HE HAD LONG LABOURED TO DESTROY.

Such is the epitaph of a weak man saved, and put to great use, by a strong God of amazing grace.

"Newton was glad he was saved!" Pastor John said.

I want to be like that.

Love that Jesus calls the weak. Love that Jesus calls people like you.

BE A REAL HUSBAND AND DAD

JONATHAN PARNELL

It was nearly 8 p.m., bedtime for the kids. I pushed my books aside and met my two little girls in their room. Thanks to their mom, I found them already lying down and the lights off. The stage was all set for me to swoop in and perform my household priestly duties—a prayer, a blessing, and a goodnight kiss. I knelt beside our four-year-old's bed to begin the routine of asking God to give her rest in Jesus, both for sleep that night and peace throughout her life. It was the stuff we prayed every night.

"Father, please give Elizabeth . . ."

"Pray for my lip!" she interrupted. It was more cute than rude. I couldn't be upset. She had hurt it playing earlier in the day, and it was still on her mind. Without missing a beat, I adeptly turned the prayer toward her little cut—sounding very spiritual, of course.

"Father, please help Elizabeth to trust you in . . ."

"My lip! My lip!" she snapped with more urgency, as if she hadn't been clear before. I chuckled inside and started again.

"Please make Elizabeth's lip to feel better . . ."

"Ask him to heal it!"

This time was different. Her tiny voice screeched from somewhere between desperation and anger. My daughter was frustrated with me, and for good reason. She could tell I was just going through the motions.

At this point, I didn't say anything. I just stopped. I couldn't move. I had been hoping to get back to those books (my time is limited, you know). But kneeling there by her bed, face in my hands, I felt the sting of a four-year-old's rebuke. It was a rebuke for how I was praying and especially how I was parenting—just going through the motions.

She had given me a plain request. Her lip hurt, and she wanted God to heal it. I had responded by praying in a fashion that was wooden and dusty, or better yet, plastic. I had walked into that room like a hollow mannequin of a dad—dressed up in all the right ways and positioned in all the right places. Yet when it came to real life, when it came to where my children live, my daughter discovered the imitation I was trying to front. Elizabeth knocked on my heart looking for faith, and all she heard was the thud of her little knuckles against an empty drum.

That was a hard night, but it was good. A glass of cold water had been poured over my head. I was finally awake and thinking.

NOW MEANS NOW

Not every seminarian is a husband and dad. But if you are, there is something you must understand: it's not that you're in seminary and happen to have a wife and children, but rather that you're a husband and dad who happens to be in seminary.

As much as deadlines and workload can tempt you to believe otherwise, parenting doesn't wait until you've finished those remaining MDiv credits. Neither does marriage—perhaps especially marriage. There are no footnotes to Ephesians 5 that qualify Paul's instructions as pending graduation. Don't be duped here. It's too costly.

Even as unique and important as the seminary experience may be, you shouldn't abdicate your family responsibilities to that "only a season" talk. If you're a husband and dad now, then you're a husband and dad *now*. What God intends for the heads of families, he intends for you, no matter what your schedule looks like or how important that paper that's due next week.

However clear your subjective sense of "a call to the ministry" may seem to you, the objective calling to be a husband and father is much clearer.

THE GOOD CHANGE IN US

In 1 Timothy 3:5, Paul writes that men who can't lead their own households well shouldn't lead in God's. This means that married seminary students don't learn how to be pastors, then figure out the home stuff later. What you do at home is more pertinent to your future ministry than the best class you'll ever take. It is even more pertinent than the exegetical gold you dig up in your studies. Every bit of gospel growth you receive by means of your theological training is aimed by God to touch all of your life. A solid seminary experience doesn't just bring a good change on this view or that, but it changes you—as a husband and as a dad, and then as a leader for the church as well.

Okay, okay! you might be thinking, *but where do I start?* Saying and believing you should be a real husband and dad is one thing; actually doing it is another. I think the best and most necessary place to start is by praying for your family. As mentioned in chapter 4, praying is the most real thing we do. And one thing you will find as you pray for your family is how you tend to rally around your specific requests. If I pray for my wife's Bible reading, I soon find myself encouraging her in it. If I pray for her to have deep friendships, I am happy to watch the kids while she gets a ladies' night out. You become committed to what you ask God to do.

There are lots of things you could pray for your family, especially your wife. Circumstances, of course, should guide your prayers to an extent. But you also need to have some things you continually ask God to do. I've written out ten such things. Though they're for your wife, these ten things are also relevant to your children with some slight modifications.

Ten Things to Pray for Your Wife

1. *God, be her God*—Be her all-satisfying treasure and all. Make her jealous for your exclusive supremacy in all her affections (Ps. 73:24–25).
2. *Increase her faith*—Give her a rock-solid confidence that your incomparable power is always wielded only for her absolute good in Christ (Rom. 8:28–30).
3. *Intensify her joy*—Fill her with a joy in you that abandons all to the riches of your grace in Jesus and that says firmly, clearly, and gladly, "I'll go anywhere and do anything if you are there" (Ex. 33:14–15).
4. *Soften her heart*—Keep her from cynicism, and make her tender to your presence in the most complicated details and the multitude of needs you've called her to meet (Heb. 13:5).

5. *Make her cherish your church*—Build relationships into her life that challenge and encourage her to walk in step with the truth of the gospel and cause her to love corporate gatherings, the Lord's Table, and the everyday life of the body (Mark 3:33–35).

6. *Give her wisdom*—Make her see dimensions of reality that I would overlook and accompany her vision with a gentle, quiet spirit that feels safe and celebrated (1 Pet. 3:4).

7. *Sustain her health*—Uphold the health of her body, and keep us from taking it for granted—all health is by blood-bought grace (Ps. 139:14).

8. *Multiply her influence*—Encourage and deepen the impact she has on our children. Give her sweet glimpses of it. Pour her out in love for our neighbors, and spark in her creative ways to engage them for Jesus's sake (John 12:24).

9. *Make her hear your voice*—Inspire her to read the Bible and accept it as it really is, your word—your very word to her where she lives, full of grace, power, and everything she needs pertaining to life and godliness (2 Pet. 1:3).

10. *Overcome her with Jesus*—Impress on her soul that she is united to him, that she is a new creature in him, that she is your daughter in him—no longer in Adam and dead to sin, but now in Christ and alive to you forever (Rom. 6:11).

LOOKING TO JESUS

No doubt, all seminarians have messed up as husbands and dads. If you're feeling guilty, take heart. There is one Husband who gave himself up for the holiness of husbands like you. There is a Shepherd who has gone before you, a Brother who is always with you, an Overseer who bore your sins in his body on the tree—including your fatherly failures—so that you might die to sin and live to righteousness. You don't have to kick the dirt in frustration at how many times you've gotten it wrong. You can look to Jesus in hope. There is healing in his wounds.

Real husbanding and fathering never gets put on hold for any season or for any degree program—no matter how hyped seminarians may be about their little pastoral callings. Way too much is at stake with your family right now to just go through the motions while you prepare for some future ministry. But as you fix your eyes on Jesus and lean desperately on him, the example he left becomes your glad path by the Spirit's power. It is then you become the real husband and dad he has called you to be.

"Pray for my lip!" my daughter might say again. And in Jesus—*in Jesus*—I'll know what to do.

KEEP BOTH EYES PEELED FOR JESUS

DAVID MATHIS

An essential mark of a solid seminary experience is continually being stunned by how everything relates to Jesus. When you look long enough, press hard enough, and feel deeply enough, you discover again and again that it all comes back to him.

The whole universe is about Jesus. The whole Bible is about Jesus. Our whole lives are designed to be about Jesus. And any seminary experience worth a dime should be all about Jesus as well. Any institution, course of study, class, professor, or text that teaches aspiring pastors any differently—explicitly or implicitly—is throwing them under the ministerial bus.

MY WORST EXPERIENCE IN SEMINARY

I remember it all too well—by far my worst moment in a seminary classroom. Normally, the minimizing of Jesus happens only implicitly in evangelical seminaries, but this time it was shockingly out in the open.

It was an intensive course during a hot summer week. The visiting professor with his Ivy League PhD sat nonchalantly on the table at the front of the class, spouting provocative comments in succession, all under the banner of hermeneutics. "Gotta till the rough soil before you can plant the high-yielding crops," he'd say. Many of his shock-jock statements were helpful, but one seemed demonic.

As he steamrolled through the biblical covenants, fitting them all nicely in his neat boxes (and PowerPoint slides), subtly muting the uniqueness and centrality of the new covenant, he finally whispered to our captive class what some of us were sensing to be latent in his system: *Jesus isn't a big deal*.

"It's all about kingdom and covenant," he said. "Jesus has an important role to play, no doubt, but in the grand scheme, it's a pretty small one. So don't go overboard making too much of Jesus." He was a tenured professor at a wonderful confessional seminary, but for a moment he seemed to embody the spirit of the Serpent in the garden.

That it was so explicit made it all the more alarming to us students. But perhaps his whispered admission did us a favor. It would have been more dangerous if the Jesus-minimizing effect of his system stayed implicit, left unnamed to ever so subtly influence the students to be centered on kingdom while diminishing the King, or to be captivated by covenant while muting the Mediator. At least, now, it was out in the open.

RESISTING THE INERTIA

Sadly, the inertia can be away from Jesus in far too many seminary classrooms. Unless the professor gives extra energy to keep relentlessly centering on him, that's the inevitable drift. There are so many other good things to learn, so many new angles to explore—and, after all, the prof's under pressure to establish his niche, get published, and all.

But even though there can be this subtle danger to move away from Jesus-centrality, the seminary experience is not worth abandoning. You simply need to go in conscious (and stay aware) of the need to unswervingly and shamelessly keep Jesus at the core—to keep both eyes peeled for him everywhere. Ferociously resist the inertia away from Jesus.

THE BIBLICAL PERVASIVENESS OF JESUS

The following doctrines and texts proved to be priceless ballast for me in steadying my soul and keeping my seminary experience on track, even when Jesus and his gospel weren't as pervasive in the classroom as they are in the Scriptures.

I. The Whole Universe Is about Jesus

Not only with respect to God the Father are all things "from him and through him and to him" (Rom. 11:36); the same can be said of God the Son. Indeed, Paul says in Colossians 1:15–20 that all things—in creation and in redemption—are in Jesus, through Jesus, and for Jesus.

Everything exists *with respect to him*. Everything exists *through him*. Everything exists *for him*. "He is before all things, and in him all things hold together" (v. 17). And he is central in our salvation, as head of the church, "that in everything he might be preeminent" (v. 18).

Perhaps no six consecutive Bible verses are more important for a distinctly Christian worldview than this passage from Colossians. All things, created and redeemed: in Jesus, through Jesus, and for Jesus. Therefore, he's worth making relentlessly pervasive in seminary education.

2. The Whole Bible Is about Jesus

If everything in the universe is in Jesus, through him, and for him, how much more, then, is everything in the Bible? We could establish this truth by good inference from Colossians 1, or we can learn it specifically from Jesus in John 5 and Luke 24, among other places.

John 5

In John 5:39–40, Jesus gives the Jewish leaders of his day a fundamental lesson in Christian hermeneutics (call it "the basic principles of the oracles of God," to use the language of Heb. 5:12), one that every reader of the Scriptures (seminarians all the more) should keep in constant view: *the Scriptures testify to him*: "You search the Scriptures because you think that in them you have eternal life; and it is they that bear witness about me, yet you refuse to come to me that you may have life."

In case we missed it, he gets more specific about the Pentateuch in verse 46: "If you believed Moses, you would believe me; for he wrote of me." Don't forget to take this truth with you to your Old Testament survey and exegesis courses.

Luke 24

This passage is the granddaddy. Jesus, fresh from his resurrection, teaches his followers that the Scriptures really have been about him all along. Beware any course in hermeneutics that doesn't get to Luke 24 fairly quickly. It doesn't get much clearer when it comes to how we should be reading our Bibles. This chapter is shamelessly Jesus-centered.

In verses 25–27, Jesus says to two of his followers on the

road to Emmaus: "O foolish ones, and slow of heart to believe all that the prophets have spoken! Was it not necessary that the Christ should suffer these things and enter into his glory?" Then Luke tells us he gave them a lesson in Bible reading with himself at the center: "And beginning with Moses and all the Prophets, he interpreted to them in all the Scriptures the things concerning himself."

Fast forward to verses 44–45:

> Then [Jesus] said to [his disciples], "These are my words that I spoke to you while I was still with you, that everything written about me in the Law of Moses and the Prophets and the Psalms must be fulfilled." Then he opened their minds to understand the Scriptures.

Spurgeon: Finding Jesus Everywhere

Given such straightforward and significant statements about the centrality of Jesus in the Scriptures, is it even possible to go overboard in finding Jesus in too many places in the Bible? Surely this approach can be abused. But as Charles Spurgeon asks, "Would it not be better to see him where he is not than to miss him where he is?"

> I love to find Jesus everywhere—not by twisting the Psalms and other Scriptures to make them speak of Christ when they do nothing of the kind, but by seeing him where he truly is. I would not err as Cocceius did, of whom they said his greatest fault was that he found Christ everywhere, but I would far rather err in his direction than have it said of me, as of another divine of the same period, that I found Christ nowhere![1]

---

[1] Charles H. Spurgeon, "Out of Egypt," Sermon No. 1675, delivered August 20, 1882. Accessed online at http://www.gospelweb.net/SpurgeonMTP28/spursermon1675.htm. Johannes Cocceius was a Dutch theologian of the seventeenth century.

3. The Whole of Our Lives Is Designed to Be about Jesus

Colossians 3:17 takes the massive scope of 1 Corinthians 10:31 and applies it explicitly to Jesus. First Corinthians 10:31: "Whether you eat or drink, or whatever you do, do all to the glory of God." Colossians 3:17: "Whatever you do, in word or deed, do everything in the name of the Lord Jesus, giving thanks to God the Father through him." You are to do everything you do in Jesus's name—and that includes seminary. How sad and sick it is to approach seminary education (of all things!) in any other way.

So keep both eyes peeled for Jesus. Relentlessly make him the explicit center of all your learning, as you keep him as the conscious focus of all your life.

CONCLUSION

Be a Christian in Seminary

DAVID MATHIS

"The point is this . . ."

I love it when Paul says that in 2 Corinthians 9:6. He makes sure he has our attention and tells it straight. Behind the reasoned prose and the rhetorical flourishes, he is about to state what he's getting at—in plain, simple, and straightforward terms: "The point is this: whoever sows sparingly will also reap sparingly, and whoever sows bountifully will also reap bountifully." That's beautifully direct.

The same humble approach helps when we take up the topic of "staying Christian" in seminary. There is so much (good) advice to be given. There are so many experiences to be relayed, warnings to be sounded, commendations to be issued, and commitments to highlight. There are particular truths to emphasize, and practical applications to give it flesh.

But when we boil it all down, what's the point? Is there something that holds all the swell advice and recommendations together? When we tell it straight and cut through all the fluff, what's at the heart of staying Christian in seminary?

The point is this: *Be a Christian in seminary*. The key to staying Christian in seminary, and in every season and avenue of life, is being one.

THE GREATEST DANGER

Perhaps the greatest danger the seminarian faces in each generation is the temptation to put some aspects of his Christianity "on hold" while he goes through this "season of preparation for ministry." Students are enticed to give themselves a pass from normal, everyday Christianity while they prepare to be instruments of normal, everyday grace to others. This is even more sad than it is ironic.

Whether it's the Tempter himself, sin, or just naiveté, the seminarian can begin to reason along these lines:

- "I don't really need a regular rhythm of personal prayer and devotional Bible intake; I'm steeped in this stuff all the time in class and in my assignments."
- "I don't really need to get deeply connected with a local church, where I can be ministered to and minister to others; my seminary community will do just fine. Besides, this is a temporary season—no reason to put any roots down here."
- "I don't really need to play the man in my household while I'm in school; my wife can hold things together temporarily and be the buckstopper while I study."

So the seminarian starts down the slope. He thinks that somehow his real-life Christianity can kick into gear once his "real life" starts on the other side of seminary. He subtly puts "on hold" his own daily pursuit of God's ongoing grace, and walking by faith in Jesus and his gospel, so he can better ready himself to introduce others to the same normal Christian life he is so strategically neglecting. So it goes.

SEMINARY IS REAL LIFE

Maybe it would help to hear that seminary *is* real life. All of life, cradle to grave, is real life in God's economy. For the Christian, there is no interlude, no pause, no "season" when we put the main things on hold to prepare for the next. There is no Christian summons to neglect securing your own oxygen mask so that you can get trained to help someone else with his or hers. You will only suffocate in the process.

How tragic it is when the seminarian, inundated with assignments and captured by the drive to succeed academically, begins to disregard the means of grace God used to cultivate his initial zeal for gospel ministry. The result is heartbreaking: seminary wrongly pursued begins to squelch the passion that led him there in the first place.

How tragic it is when the committed seminarian is inattentive in ministering first to his wife and kids because he's in a season of "preparing for ministry." The apostle Paul wouldn't be impressed, but would say such a one "has denied the faith and is worse than an unbeliever" (1 Tim. 5:8).

How tragic it is when the diligent seminarian begins to be impressed with how much he's learning, how much he knows, and what a great gift he'll be to the church on the other side of graduation. The apostle would remind him: "This 'knowledge' puffs up, but love builds up. If anyone imagines that he knows something, he does not yet know as he ought to know" (1 Cor. 8:1–2).

LESS ABOUT SEMINARY, MORE ABOUT CHRISTIANITY

Follow the trail of "staying Christian" in seminary long enough and you'll realize it's less about what a special season seminary is and more about what Christianity is in every season of life, in every age of church history, and in every place on the planet.

Staying Christian in seminary is about staying Christian in general.

And the way to stay Christian in the long run is be a Christian every day. Walk daily in light of God's fascinating and extraordinary grace to us in the gospel. Fully reliant on God's Spirit, go deep in God's word, among God's people. Keep both eyes peeled for Jesus—not only in the Scriptures, but in every avenue of existence. Fight pride. Serve your wife. Be eager to meet the needs of others, to minister and be ministered to by fellow believers, and to share the gospel and yourself with those who don't yet know him.

There is no holding pattern for the Christian flight. God's calling to seminary doesn't trump, but complements, his calling for you, by his grace, to daily be the kind of husband, father, friend, and follower of Jesus that you hope your post-seminary formal ministry will one day produce.

RECOMMENDED READING

Further Resources for Staying Christian in Seminary

Frame, John. "Learning at Jesus' Feet: A Case for Seminary Training." Available online at http://www.frame-poythress.org/frame_articles /2003Learning.htm.

Frame, John. "Studying Theology as a Servant of Jesus." Available online at http://www.frame-poythress.org/studying-theology-as-a-servant -of-jesus/.

Kapic, Kelly M. *A Little Book for Young Theologians: Why and How to Study Theology.* Downers Grove, IL: InterVarsity Press, 2012.

Thielicke, Helmut. *A Little Exercise for Young Theologians.* Translated by Charles L. Taylor. Grand Rapids: Eerdmans, 1962.

Warfield, Benjamin B. *The Religious Life of Theological Students.* Phillipsburg, NJ: Presbyterian & Reformed, 1983.

ACKNOWLEDGMENTS

We thank God for the remarkable harmony that emerged in the process of coauthoring this book. Although each of the chapters is specific to one of us, the message of this book is one of full and happy agreement.

We thank God for Justin Taylor at Crossway, who approached us with the idea of growing our little blog series on staying Christian in seminary into this little book.

Thank you to the partners across the Web who participated in the #HSXS initiative in April 2012: Nathan Akin, Bruce Ashford, Denny Burk, Nathan Finn, Jim Hamilton, Michael Horton, Andy Naselli, Dane Ortlund, Ray Ortlund, Burk Parsons, Matt Smethurst, and Trevin Wax. We've put links to their posts on staying Christian in seminary at www.desiringGod.org/seminary.

Thank you to our friends and daily ministry partners (and bosses!) at Desiring God. In particular, thanks to Jon Bloom and Josh Etter for your smiling support of this project from the outset. Thank you, Tony Reinke, for your encouragement and help. And thank you, John Piper, for the foreword and for the indelible impression you have left on our lives and all our pages.

I (Jonathan) thank my wife, Melissa, who has walked with me through a lot of school, nourished me with laughter, and once said to me, "You can come up with a lot of things you can't do when you keep your eyes on yourself." I love you.

I (David) thank my remarkable wife, Megan, who bears all things, believes all things, hopes all things, endures all things.

Under God, I don't know if I could have stayed Christian parenting twin boys except for my Wonder Woman. Thank you for holding on summer after muggy summer—the worst possible time of year to pitch our tent in Orlando—so I could get the on-campus hours at RTS. You are patient and kind. I love you.

Finally, and most of all, we thank Jesus—our matchless Savior, peerless Lord, and priceless Treasure—who took our place on the cross, defeated death for our sake, ever lives to be our Life and Joy, and keeps us Christian by his Spirit.

SCRIPTURE INDEX

SUBJECT INDEX